We are born pure

*Dedicated to my Papa, with God in Heaven
and my grandchildren next to me.
Max, Michael, Jordan and Dani
always bring me back
when I get lost.*

*Carrie, my daughter, is my Princess.
David, my son, I wish
for all mothers to have.*

~

Simply
Meditate

First edition

*Library of Congress
ISBN 978-0-9987395-0-2*

Published by Estherleon Schwartz

*Contact: esterleon@estherleon.com
www.estherleon.com*

*Book design and typesetting by Michael Rosen
Cover design by Rozanne Taucher*

*Also by Estherleon Schwartz:
Tears of Stone and My Deal With God*

Printed in the United States of America

Each meditation begins with...

"I LIFT MY EYES AND HEART UPWARD." It is a memory, a vision, words imprinted in my heart for always, when my Papa lifted his eyes upward and uttered, "Save my daughter and she will always serve you." It was 1945... we were escaping from the Nazis. And I knew one day, that vision and those words and more... would have a purpose.

My journey to Mindfulness Meditations is made possible through the artistic sensitivity of my long time friend and creative partner, musician/producer, Ivor Pyres. Together, we began live Mindfulness Music Meditations, woven with sacred sound, poetry and spoken word - which led to this book.

I feel teaching gratitude in schools is the most important value to instill. I developed the Gratitude Buddie Circle to follow the Pledge of Allegiance to dispel bullying, anti-Semitism and hate. Kids become buddies and care for each other and their communities through sharing and gratefulness. I wish this to be implemented in all schools. ASAP.

Special thanks go to Rozanne Taucher and Michael Rosen for their wordsmith contributions. I wish for all to have friends like these.

I hope to meet you all one day when we do our live Mindfulness Music Meditations or our book signings.

...e

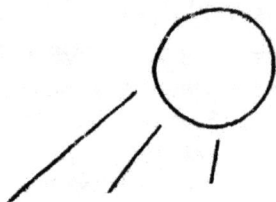

**...I LIFT MY EYES AND HEART UPWARD
I SLOWLY TAKE A DEEP...DEEP WONDROUS
BREATH WHICH SUSTAINS ME**

I feel a Presence
a Calm that fills my being

I am Grateful

I am Alive

A brand new Day
A brand new Moment

Expect the unexpected
Miracles around the corner

Now Rock around the Clock!

---

*When you repeat this at will, it gives power to the words
and they will serve you well.*

I am Grateful

I am Grateful

I am Grateful

**...I LIFT MY EYES AND HEART UPWARD
I SLOWLY TAKE A DEEP...DEEP WONDROUS
BREATH WHICH SUSTAINS ME**

I feel a Presence
a Calm that fills my being

I gently inhale...another deep wondrous Breath
that gives me Clarity

I simply exhale...Clouded thoughts

*When you repeat this at will, it gives power to the words
and they will serve you well.*

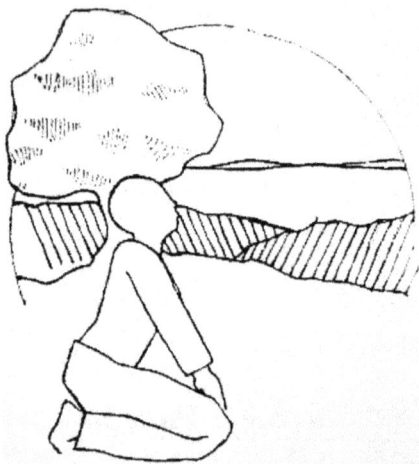

**...I LIFT MY EYES AND HEART UPWARD
I SLOWLY TAKE A DEEP...DEEP WONDROUS
BREATH WHICH SUSTAINS ME**

I feel a Presence
a Calm that fills my being

I gently inhale another deep wondrous
Breath of Purpose
I simply exhale distortion

I am Mindful of my thoughts
I have Purpose

Calm settles over me

All is Possible
Gratitude rests in my Being

*When you repeat this at will, it gives power to the words
and they will serve you well.*

I am filled with thank-yous

I am filled with thank-yous

I am filled with thank-yous

**...I LIFT MY EYES AND HEART UPWARD
I SLOWLY TAKE A DEEP...DEEP WONDROUS
BREATH WHICH SUSTAINS ME**

I feel a Presence
a Calm that fills my being

A Presence
a Calm giving me Mindfulness
an awareness even my toothbrush
always serving my teeth for Health

It too, has an inanimate Spirit Life
Each moment in time

I am more Aware
I am more Aware
I am more Aware

*When you repeat this at will, it gives power to the words
and they will serve you well.*

**...I LIFT MY EYES AND HEART UPWARD
I SLOWLY TAKE A DEEP...DEEP WONDROUS
BREATH WHICH SUSTAINS ME**

I feel a Presence
a Calm that fills my being
A Presence
a Calm giving me Mindfulness
an Awareness, each moment in time

To be Mindful of the Bird that
sings good morning to Me

I am Mindful

I am Aware

I am

*When you repeat this at will, it gives power to the words
and they will serve you well.*

All is good

All is good

All is good

...I LIFT MY EYES AND HEART UPWARD
I SLOWLY TAKE A DEEP...DEEP WONDROUS
BREATH WHICH SUSTAINS ME

I feel a Presence
a Calm that fills my being

I gently inhale Compassion
I simply exhale unkindness

I see with my Heart tho' my eyes are closed
I see a new Light with my eyes open

*When you repeat this at will, it gives power to the words
and they will serve you well.*

–Dani

...I LIFT MY EYES AND HEART UPWARD
I SLOWLY TAKE A DEEP...DEEP WONDROUS
BREATH WHICH SUSTAINS ME

I feel a Presence
a Calm that fills my being
A Presence of Calm surrounds me
This Moment in time
A Scent, I feel the touch
Of the satin Rose

I am calmly bursting with Calm
I gently inhale another deep wondrous
Breath of Joy

Connecting with myself and Earth

*When you repeat this at will, it gives power to the words
and they will serve you well.*

**...I LIFT MY EYES AND HEART UPWARD
I SLOWLY TAKE A DEEP...DEEP WONDROUS
BREATH WHICH SUSTAINS ME**

I feel a Presence
a Calm that fills my being

I gently Inhale all that gives me Balance
I plant a Tree

Each day I hug my Tree
It blooms that Lemon scent

I simply inhale, inhale and inhale

I am filled with Joy of Scent
I am filled with Scent of Joy

I am Happy
I am Happy
I am Really Happy

*When you repeat this at will, it gives power to the words
and they will serve you well.*

You're covered

**...I LIFT MY EYES AND HEART UPWARD
I SLOWLY TAKE A DEEP...DEEP WONDROUS
BREATH WHICH SUSTAINS ME**

I feel a Presence
a Calm that fills my being

I simply Exhale all that stings

A Presence that says, "All is good."

Slowly keep breathing in the pure fresh air
Pureness enlightens you

You are Mindful
Of every sense of your pores

Simply look Upward
Morning, Noon and Night

*When you repeat this at will, it gives power to the words
and they will serve you well.*

**...I LIFT MY EYES AND HEART UPWARD
I SLOWLY TAKE A DEEP...DEEP WONDROUS
BREATH WHICH SUSTAINS ME**

I feel a Presence
a Calm that fills my being
I simply Inhale more deep wondrous Breath

My Soul, my Being is filled with wonder
Like the gentle stream
that flows and flows
Am I there?

As Calm as pure water, as pure as snow
All from Above
I am here in this mindful moment
in Bliss in Bliss in Bliss

I am Blessed

*When you repeat this at will, it gives power to the words
and they will serve you well.*

I'm OK

You're OK

All OK for now

**...I LIFT MY EYES AND HEART UPWARD
I SLOWLY TAKE A DEEP...DEEP WONDROUS
BREATH WHICH SUSTAINS ME**

I feel a Presence
a Calm that fills my being
I simply Inhale more deep wondrous Breath
I feel connected to Me, to You

Filled with Calm
and Appreciation
For another deep wondrous
Breath of Life

I connect
I connect
I connect

*When you repeat this at will, it gives power to the words
and they will serve you well.*

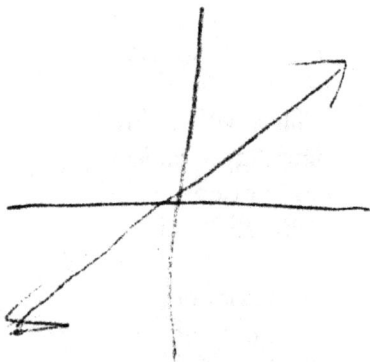

–Dani

**...I LIFT MY EYES AND HEART UPWARD
I SLOWLY TAKE A DEEP...DEEP WONDROUS
BREATH WHICH SUSTAINS ME**

I feel a Presence
a Calm that fills my being
I gently Inhale more wondrous deep
pure Breath of Calm

I simply exhale distractions

Enough is Enough

*When you repeat this at will, it gives power to the words
and they will serve you well.*

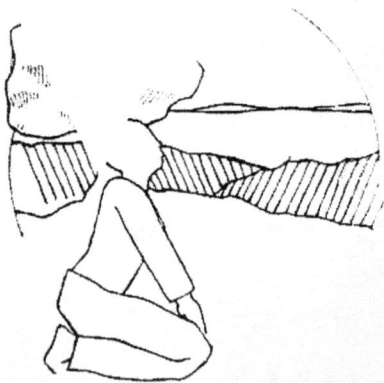

...I LIFT MY EYES AND HEART UPWARD
THE PRESENCE OF CALM
IS IMPRINTED INTO MY BEING

I slowly take a deep...deep wondrous Breath
which sustains me

Hidden Wisdom lies within the deep
wondrous pure Breath

I wish this for all
I wish this
I wish

*When you repeat this at will, it gives power to the words
and they will serve you well.*

I am Mindful

I am Mindful

I am Mindful

**...I LIFT MY EYES AND HEART UPWARD
I SLOWLY TAKE A DEEP...DEEP WONDROUS
BREATH WHICH SUSTAINS ME**

I feel a Presence
a Calm that fills my being

I simply exhale all Minutia
I gently inhale a deep wondrous
Breath of Mindfulness

I am Aware of my Thoughts

I am Aware of my Thoughts

I am Aware of my Thoughts

---

*When you repeat this at will, it gives power to the words
and they will serve you well.*

...I LIFT MY EYES AND HEART UPWARD
I SLOWLY TAKE A DEEP...DEEP WONDROUS
BREATH WHICH SUSTAINS ME

I feel a Presence
a Calm that fills my being

I see the Sunset
In this Moment of Time
I am Grateful I can just...Be

Just Be

Just Be

Just Be

*When you repeat this at will, it gives power to the words
and they will serve you well.*

Hallelujah
...*e*

...I LIFT MY EYES AND HEART UPWARD
I SLOWLY TAKE A DEEP...DEEP WONDROUS
BREATH WHICH SUSTAINS ME

I feel a Presence
a Calm that fills my being

A deep wondrous Breath sighs in Awe

All Is Good

All Is Good

All Is Good

---

*When you repeat this at will, it gives power to the words
and they will serve you well.*

I am Blessed

I am Blessed

I am Blessed

**...I LIFT MY EYES AND HEART UPWARD
I SLOWLY TAKE A DEEP...DEEP WONDROUS
BREATH WHICH SUSTAINS ME**

I feel a Presence
a Calm that fills my being

Beautiful thoughts surround Me

I feel Grateful

I feel Blessed

I feel Peaceful

---

*When you repeat this at will, it gives power to the words
and they will serve you well.*

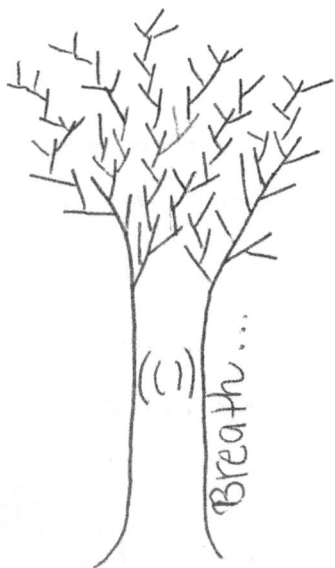

Breath...

–Dani

**...I LIFT MY EYES AND HEART UPWARD
I SLOWLY TAKE A DEEP...DEEP WONDROUS
BREATH WHICH SUSTAINS ME**

I feel a Presence
a Calm that fills my being

The Breath of Hope
The Breath of Faith

A Presence of Calm surrounds me

with Grace

with Wholeness

with Divineness

...You're home free

---

*When you repeat this at will, it gives power to the words
and they will serve you well.*

**...I LIFT MY EYES AND HEART UPWARD
I SLOWLY TAKE A DEEP...DEEP WONDROUS
BREATH WHICH SUSTAINS ME**

I feel a Presence
a Calm that fills my being

In the Silence I am Mindful of my Being

Rest with the Night

Simply rest, my friend

Rest

Rest

Rest

*When you repeat this at will, it gives power to the words
and they will serve you well.*

...I LIFT MY EYES AND HEART UPWARD
I SLOWLY TAKE A DEEP...DEEP WONDROUS
BREATH WHICH SUSTAINS ME

I feel a Presence
a Calm that fills my being

A Presence Of Calm Surrounds Me
I gently inhale more of a deep
precious breath of Calm

I simply exhale all YUK

All is good

All is good

All is good

---

*When you repeat this at will, it gives power to the words
and they will serve you well.*

**...I LIFT MY EYES AND HEART UPWARD
I SLOWLY TAKE A DEEP...DEEP WONDROUS
BREATH WHICH SUSTAINS ME**

I feel a Presence
a Calm that fills my being

A Presence of Calm surrounds Me
I gently inhale a deep
wondrous Breath of Divine order

I simply exhale CLUTTER

I am

I am

I am

———— • ————

*When you repeat this at will, it gives power to the words
and they will serve you well.*

**...I LIFT MY EYES AND HEART UPWARD
I SLOWLY TAKE A DEEP...DEEP WONDROUS
BREATH WHICH SUSTAINS ME**

I feel a Presence
a Calm that fills my being

I gently inhale a deep wondrous
breath of Silence

I simply exhale the excess Chatter in my head

Lifting your eyes and heart upward works

Now I can really rest

Now I can really rest

Now I can really Be

*When you repeat this at will, it gives power to the words
and they will serve you well.*

...I LIFT MY EYES AND HEART UPWARD
I SLOWLY TAKE A DEEP...DEEP WONDROUS
BREATH WHICH SUSTAINS ME

I feel a Presence
a Calm that fills my being

I gently inhale a deep wondrous
Breath of mystical Silence

I simply exhale needless Thoughts

So it shall be

So it shall be

So it shall be

---

*When you repeat this at will, it gives power to the words
and they will serve you well.*

....I LIFT MY EYES AND HEART UPWARD
I SLOWLY TAKE A DEEP...DEEP WONDROUS
BREATH WHICH SUSTAINS ME

I feel a Presence
a Calm that fills my being

I simply inhale a precious wondrous
Breath of Blessings
I am Blessed
You are Blessed

My Being rests with the World

My Being rests with Life

My Being rests with my pure born Self

*When you repeat this at will, it gives power to the words
and they will serve you well.*

*Your precious feelings and words,
from your own pen to paper,
have power.*

*Your precious feelings and words,
from your own pen to paper,
have power.*

**...I LIFT MY EYES AND HEART UPWARD
A PRESENCE OF CALM FILLS MY SOUL**

Pray, Dance, Sing with Chocolate

And *Simply Meditate With Giggles*
(book 2 coming soon...)

your friend...*e*

www.ingramcontent.com/pod-product-compliance
Lightning Source LLC
Chambersburg PA
CBHW021223020426
42331CB00003B/444